NATIONAL GEOGRAPHIC

Our Clubhouse

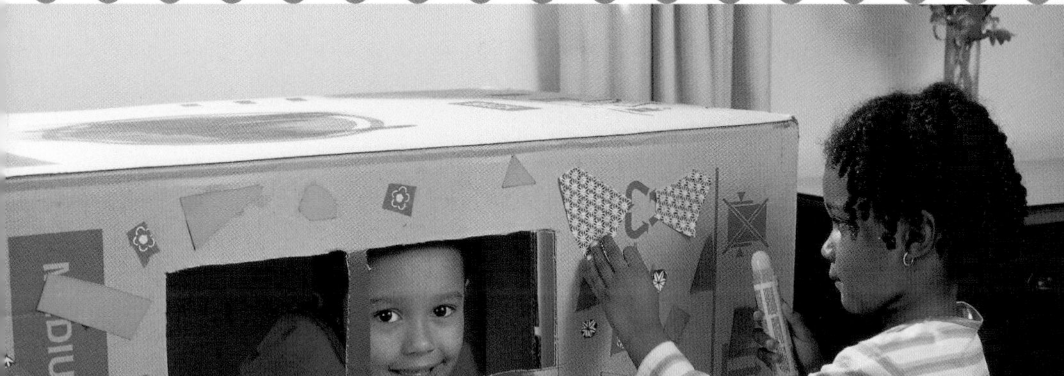

Mark Macey

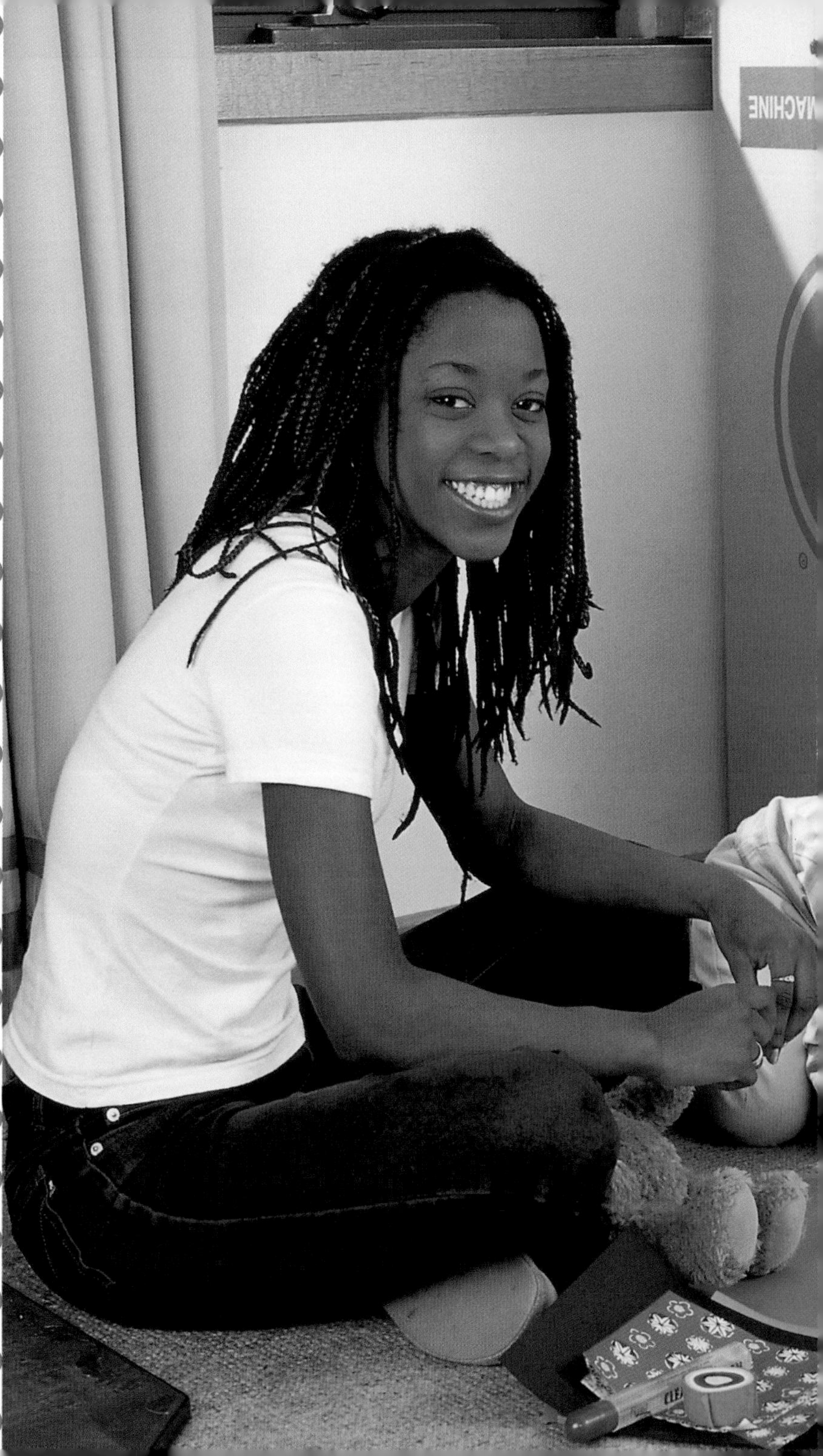

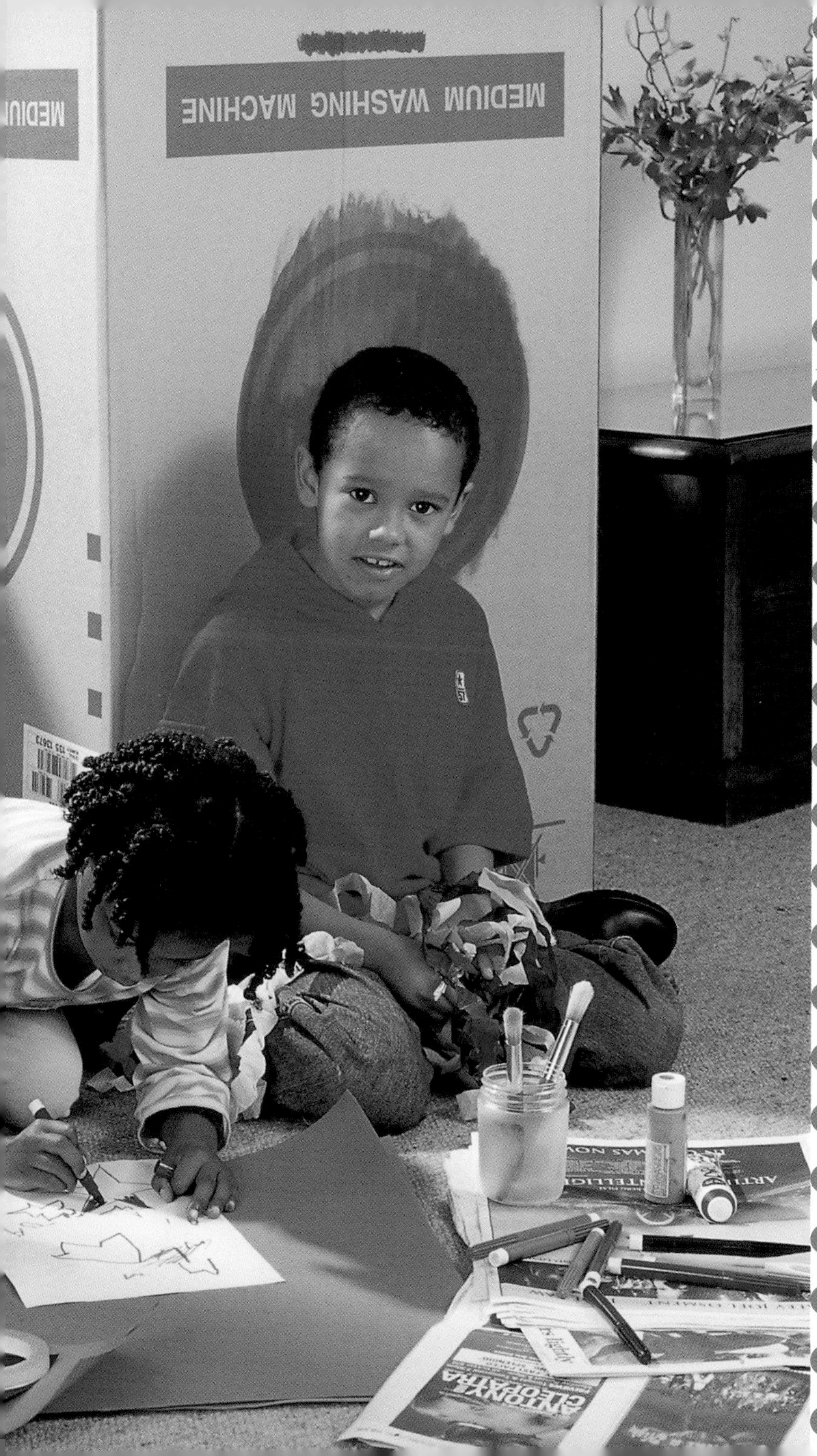
MEDIUM WASHING MACHINE

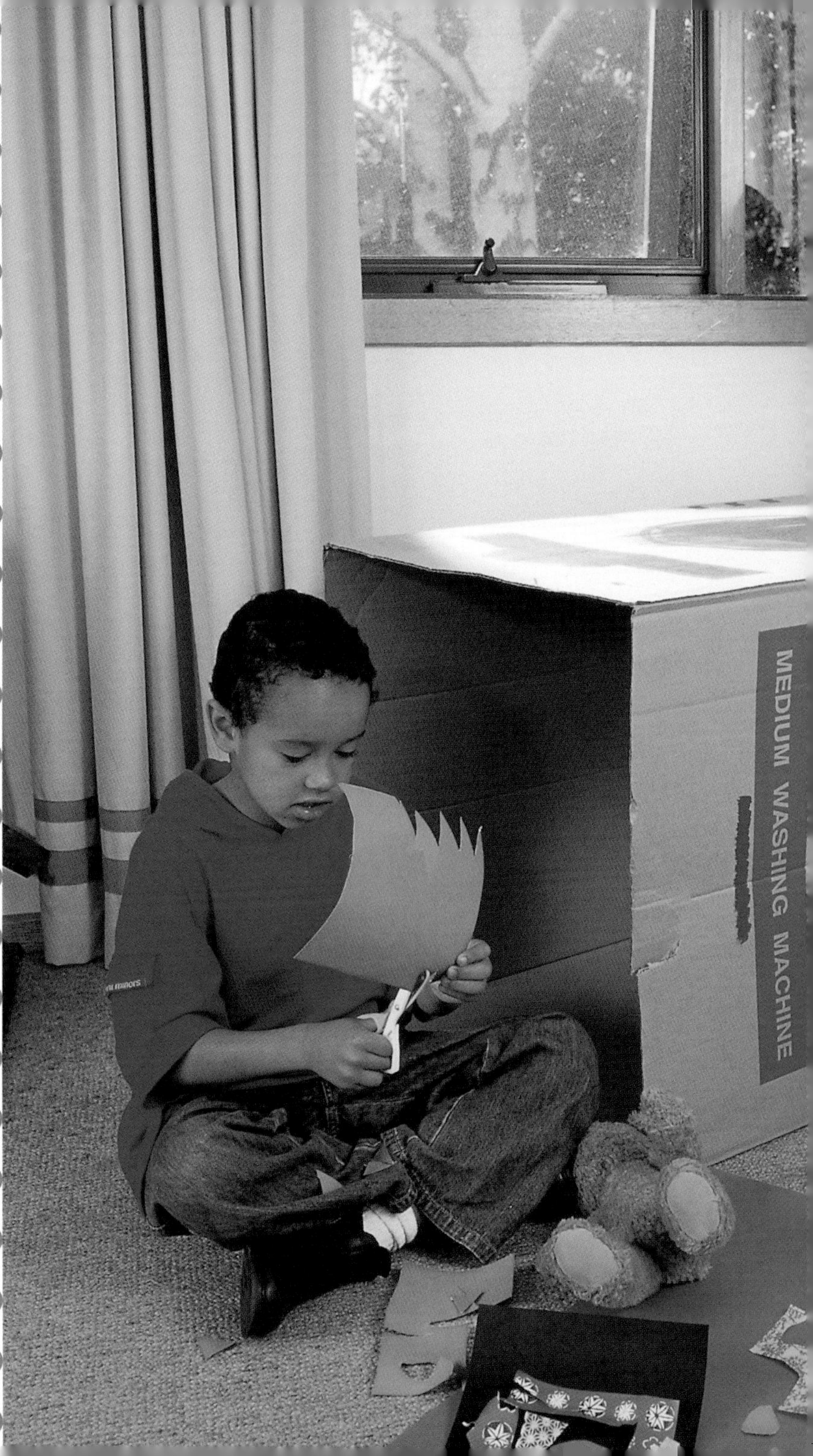
MEDIUM WASHING MACHINE

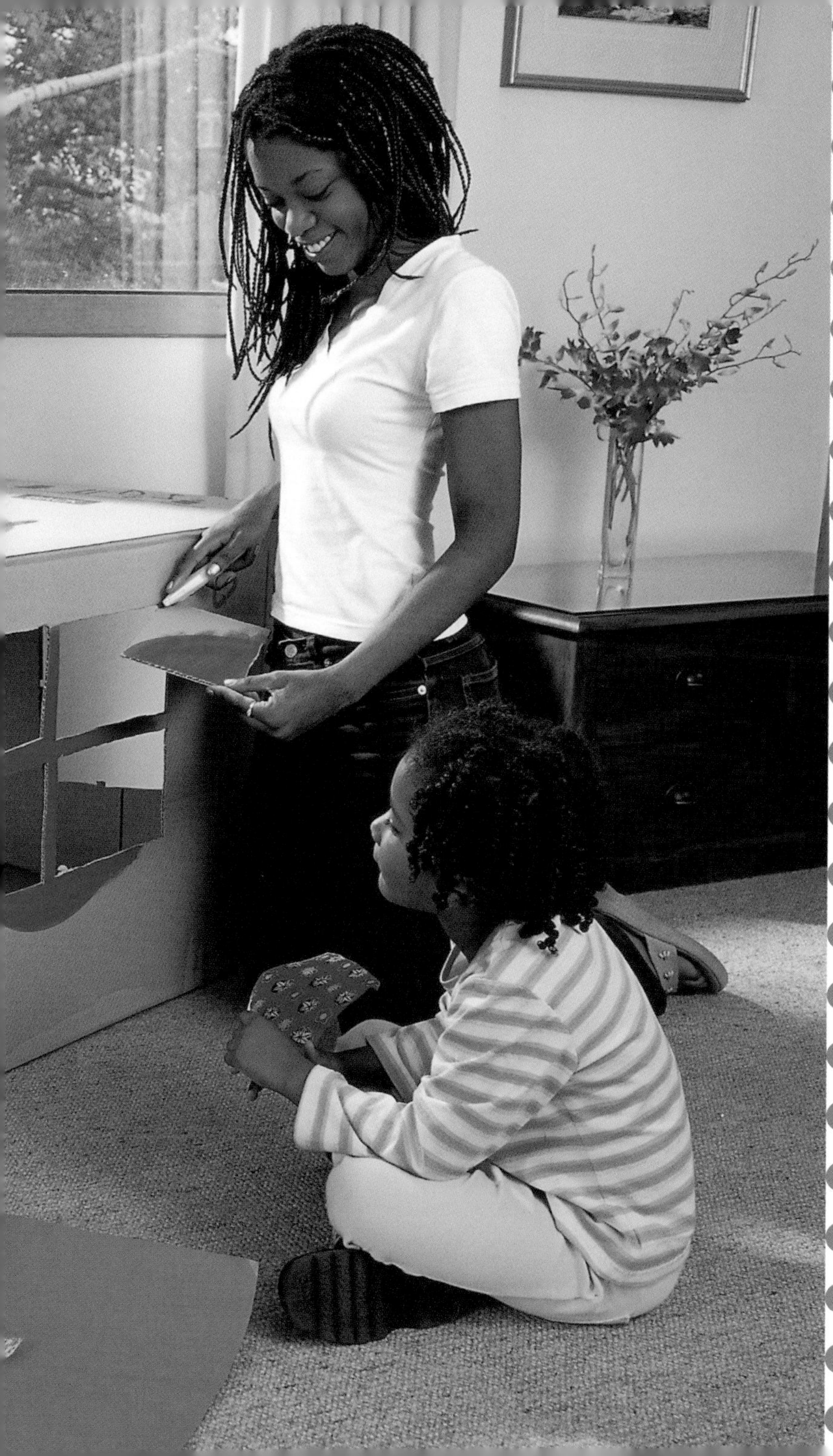

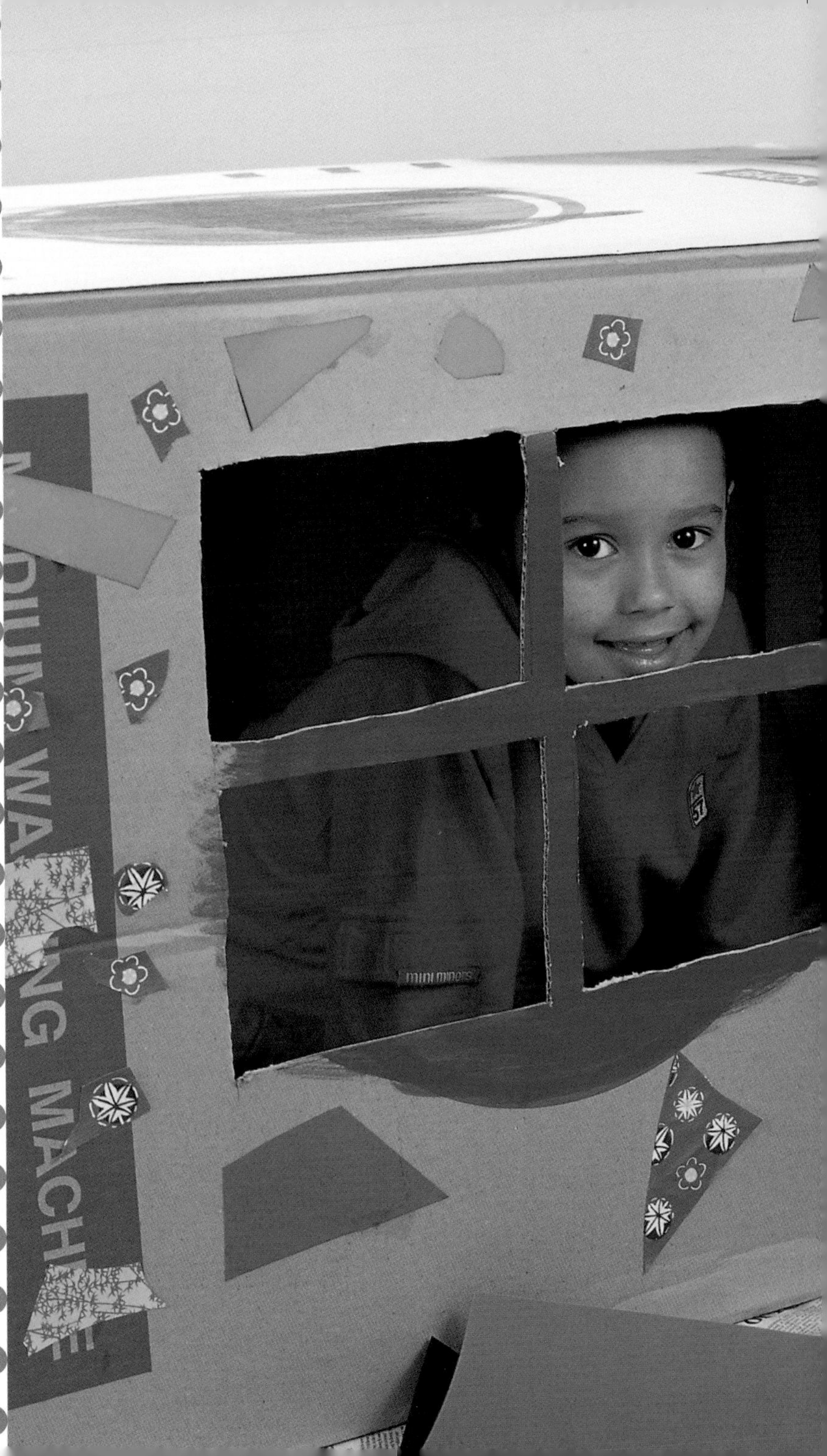

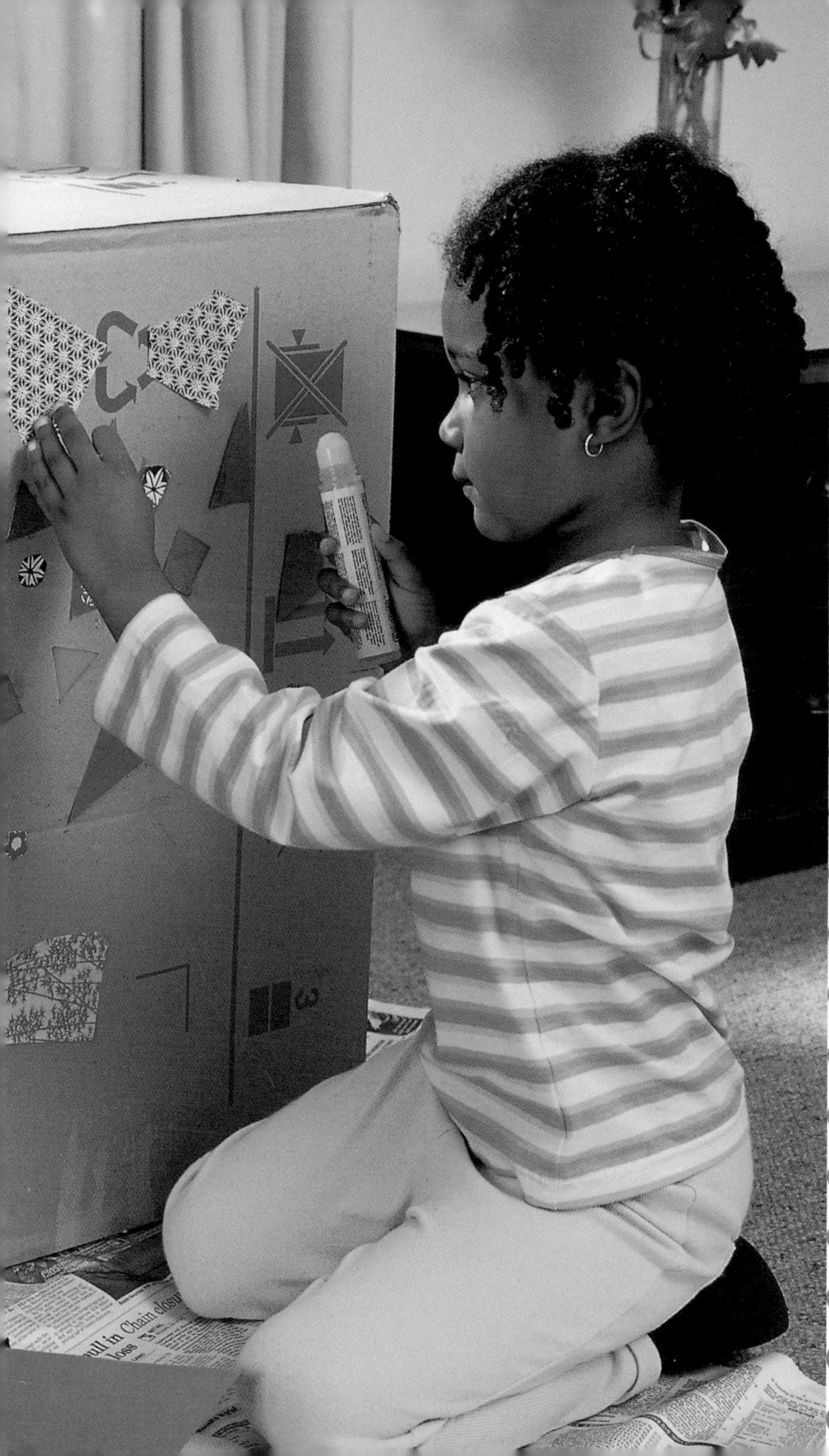

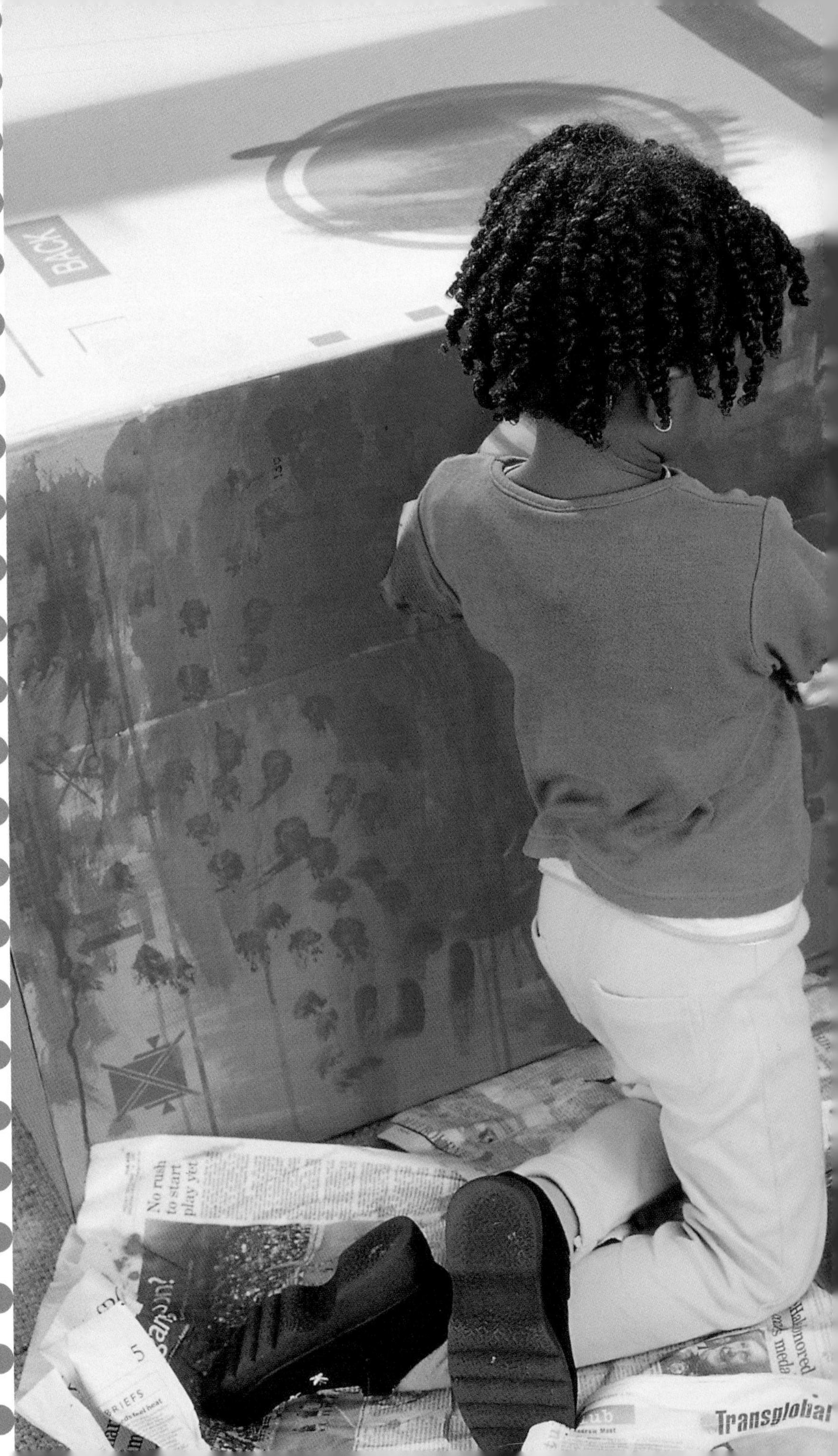
BACK
No rush to start play yet
Transglobal

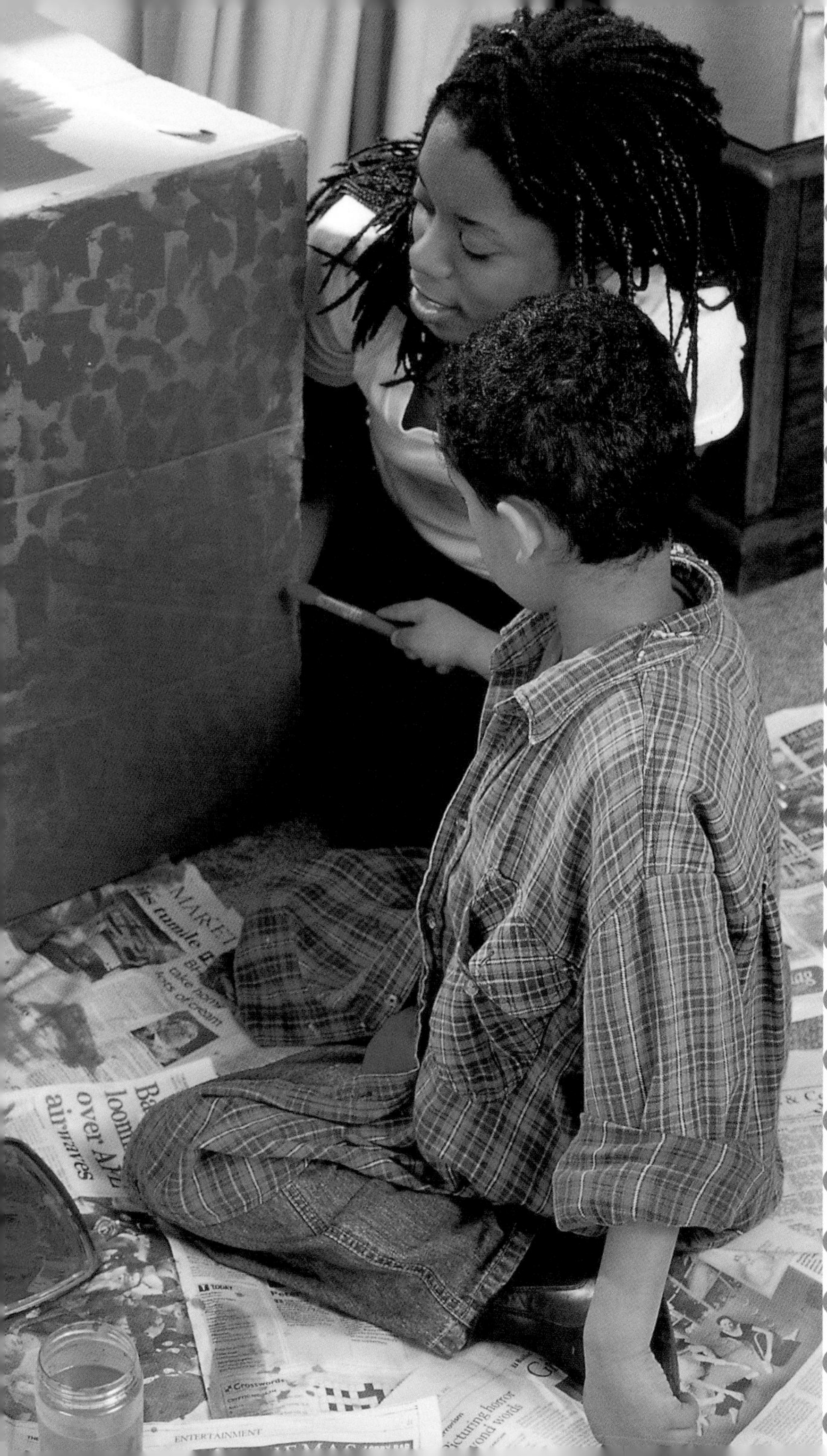

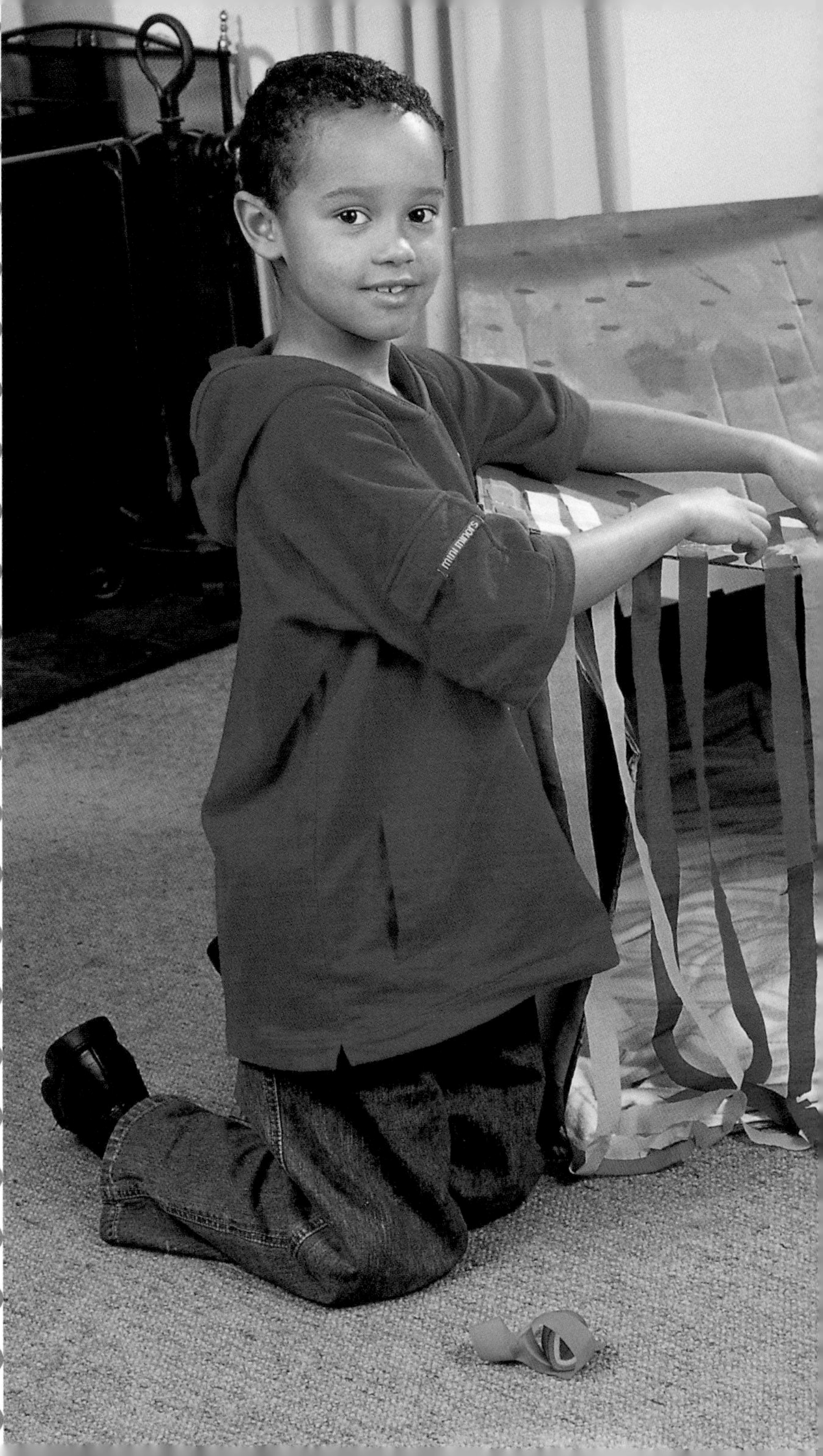

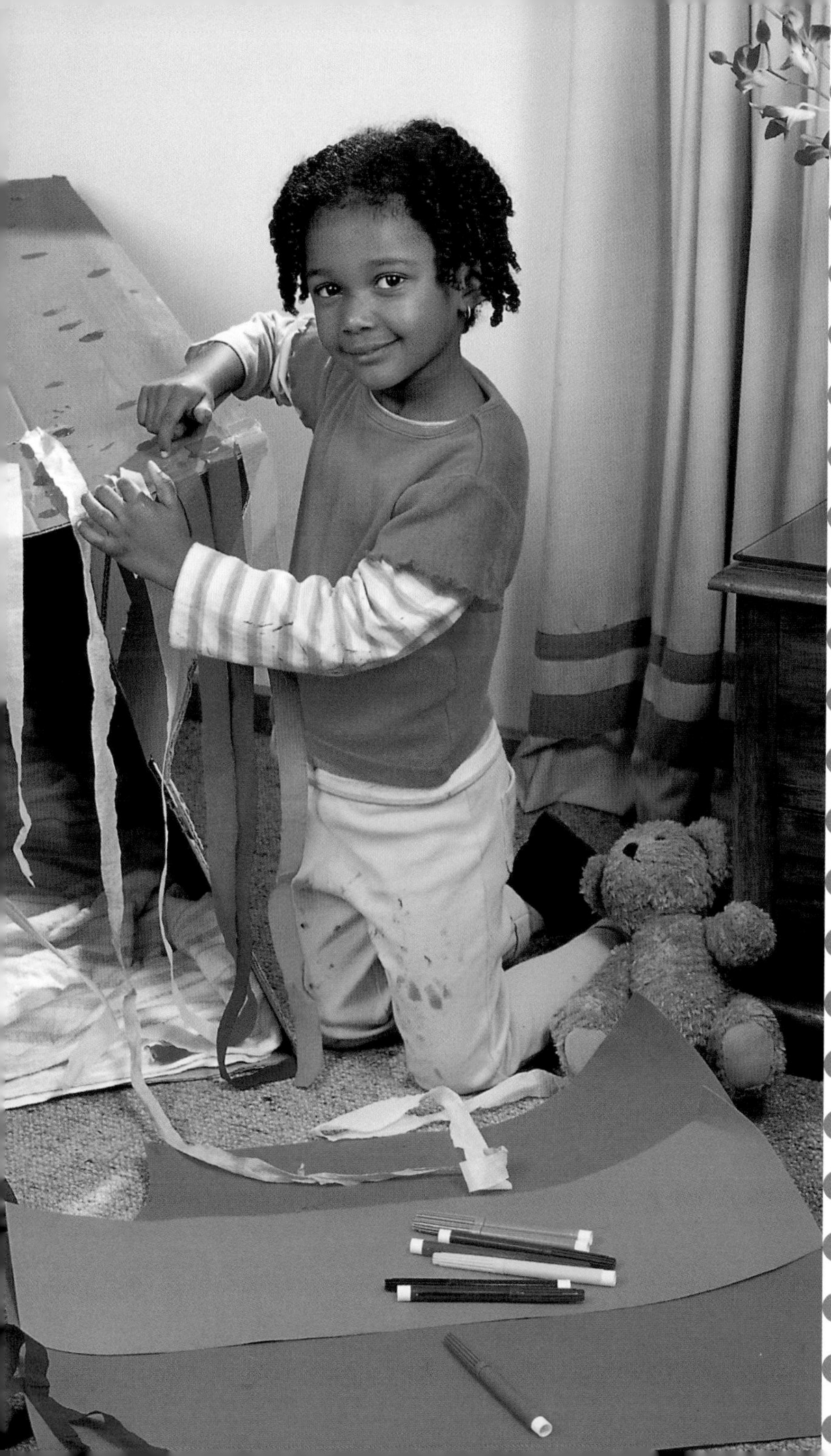

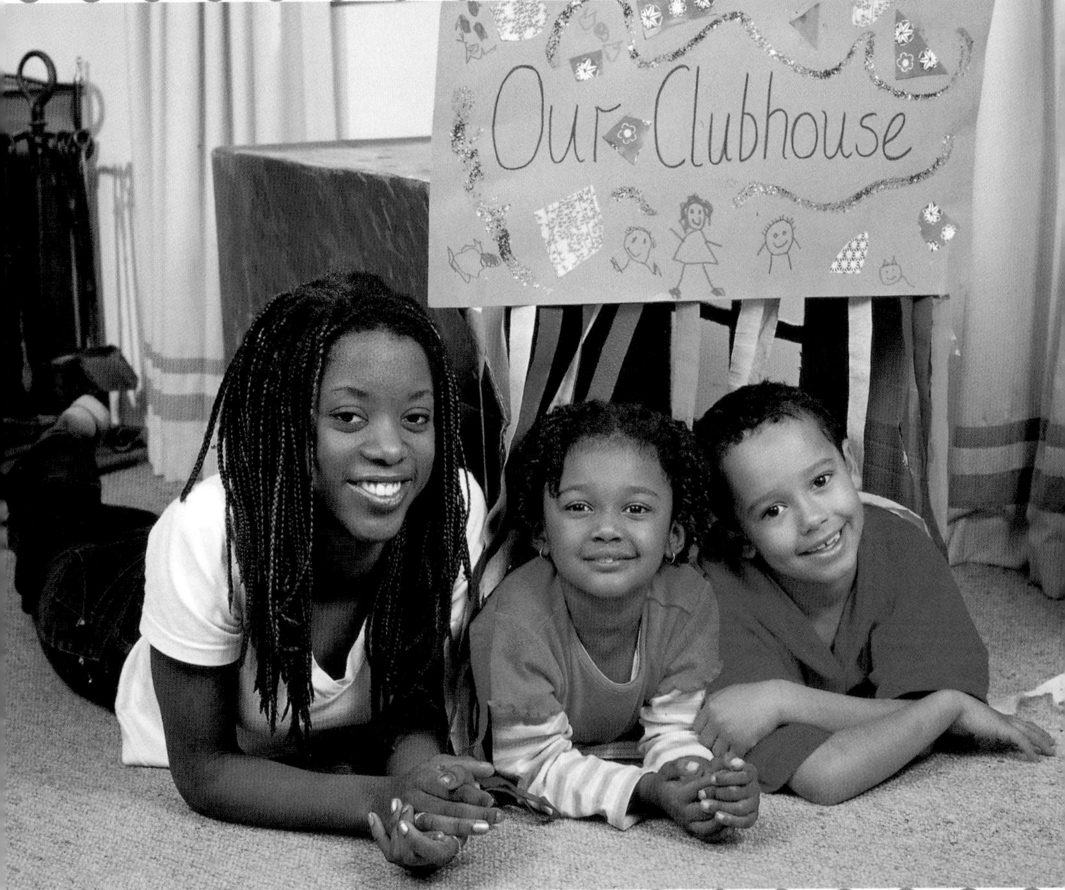
Our Clubhouse